for Real?

True life stories through
the Lens of the Bible

FOR REAL?

True life stories through the lens of the Bible

For all trade orders and bulk purchase
please contact us on: +234809 044 7764
tamunonye@gmail.com

Photo Credit: Arinze Orajiaka
Cover Design: Fabia Batubo

Printed in Nigeria by

MIND-QUEST

Email: mindquest12@gmail.com
Tel: 0803 551 6978

Table of Contents

Dedication

I dedicate this book to my Lord and
Savior, Jesus Christ Who is the
essence of my being and Who colors
my life so beautifully.

Appreciation

First of all, I thank the Almighty God Who gave me life and made this writing possible.

Thank you, dad, Apostle Geoffrey D. Numbere (of blessed memory) and thank you mum, Pastor Dr. Nonyem Numbere for loving me and bringing me up right.

My beloved husband, Victor and my children, I love you so much. Thank you for all the love and support you pour and lavish on me.

My wonderful family, my siblings "The Numbere boys", "The GRA Family" and my inlaws. I could not have asked for a better family, there is never a dull moment with you.

My editorial team: my mum, Pastor Nonyem Numbere, Toki Numbere (Editor-in-chief), Ego Akintoye, Erebi Ndoni, Dr. Mrs. Eunice Ajie, thank you.

My spiritual leader, Pastor and Pastor Mrs. Isaac Olori, thank you mum and dad for always being there for me.

Thank you, Elsie Francis for tagging me in the Facebook Challenge. What started as fun, is now a book and I trust it will bless everyone who reads it. I also appreciate my cousin, Numbere, Apainaemi E. who gave this book its captivating title, and my "For Real" team.   You rock!

To my beloved mentors, pastors, colleagues, aunties, uncles and friends, thank you. For some of you, I am unable to write your names directly, but when you read my story, you know I am talking about you. Thank you so much for all you have done and continue to do. Thank you for being part of my story. God bless you in more ways than you can imagine.

I love you all.

Prologue

This book is what I call a "Beautiful Accident". It all started on August 17, 2020 when my friend, Elsie Francis tagged me in a 10-day challenge on Facebook. The challenge was to share a bible passage that means a lot to me, every day for 10 days.

So, for 10 days I shared the personal stories that made those verses stand out, and the lessons I learned. A lot of people asked me to compile them, and this little book is the result. I call it a beautiful accident because I never planned for it. I was at the time working on (what I thought would be) my first book to be released in 2021 and also my first single, titled "Almighty" but this sprung out of nowhere and I just had to go with the flow.

On the next page is a message from my parents, written on the bible they gifted me on my graduation from the university. I have found it to be true. Jesus Christ is my Lord and Savior; He has been my life and my light; I have always drawn strength from Him; He has sustained me and still sustains me. I invite you to accept Him as your Lord too, He will give your life a meaning.

Also, it has been deliberately written with Nigerian lexicon. The reader must have an idea of Nigerian slangs and local parlance to fully enjoy the humor in the book.

A friend told me there is no such thing as an accident with God, and I believe this is true. I trust that you will be blessed as you go through my little stories.

Friday 14th March, 2003.

TAMMI beloved,

On this auspicious occasion of your graduation with 2nd Class Upper Division, Mummy and I have thought hard and long what would be the best gift from us to you. We finally settled on this one gift — THE WORD OF GOD (BIBLE) We brought you up with it; we sustained you with it, and we trust it will sustain you the rest of your days on earth. Open it daily for in it you will find all that you will need to live on and live by.

CONGRATULATIONS!

Daddy & Mummy

CHAPTER 1

A Present Help In Time of Trouble

*God is our refuge and strength,
a very present help in trouble.
Psalm 46:1*

G rowing up, our home, even though large, was full of love and warmth. We had between fifteen to twenty people in our home at any given time; some of whom we had no direct blood relationship. Interestingly, my parents treated every single one equally. The bond and love remains even today, extending to our children as well.

During the early '90s, the main waste disposal system in our city consisted of large bins (called SULO) placed at every street junction for residents to empty refuse. They would then be picked up by big waste disposal trucks.

Unfortunately, like most initiatives in Nigeria, this deteriorated quickly and we had to walk long distances just to drop our refuse at designated points. The bins at this location, if at all they were there, were too few to handle the entire district. As children, every other day, we had the chore of taking our bin on the one-kilometre walk for disposal. We had a lot of fun, playing and holding races on the road.

On this particular day, by the time we got there the bins were full, and there was refuse all over the place. There, were chatting away and having fun as usual, as we proceeded to drop the bin bags by the bins.

Next thing we heard, "FREEZE"! After watching so many movies, we knew what to do! Hands went straight up in the air. The "officer" put his hand in his pocket as though he was concealing a weapon. I froze, literally. "Freeze or I shoot", he shouted!

They were the Environmental Sanitation Authority personnel, and they rounded us up into their vehicle. It was so jam packed that some of us had to sit on the floor. We were under arrest for inappropriate disposal of refuse. My mind was racing, I was scared silly. My parents would be worried, how would they know? They would think we were lost, all of us were on the bus.

Anyway, still in that mood of movies, I picked up courage and told the man seated close to me: "I want to make a phone call". The man said, "*eh*[1]?" I said, "Phone, I want to call my parents". He just looked at me, shook his head, "Who is this *ajebutter*[2]? Telephone?"

---

[1] What?
[2] Someone who has lived an expensive life

You see, there were no mobile phones at the time. Back then, having a telephone was a luxury. My parents had one; to dial, you would put your finger in and turn each number. Families used to schedule visits to our house to call their relatives overseas, and some of them did not even know how to hold the phone or hang up correctly. We had fun listening to them scream... "Helloooo!", "Sisterrr!", in excitement at hearing the voice of their loved ones! Good times!

So here I was, under arrest! And no option for a phone call! But God was ahead. One of my cousins, unknown to us, had escaped. Our very own Usain Bolt! He *"picked race[3]"* and ran *"440"* all the way back home without stopping. Yep! Like Job's servants, "only I have escaped to tell you!" He broke the news to my parents. We lived in the Church premises called the Base and the place went agog on hearing what had happened.

Ghen Ghen[4]! If you want trouble, touch any of us! My parents will rip you apart, literally. My parents jumped into the car, dad at the driving seat. You see, dad at the

____

[3] Ran

[4] Action

driving seat is a story on its own, nothing short of James Bond '007. The others jumped into the bus and followed behind. They headed straight to the Environmental Sanitation office.

All I know is that as soon as we got to their office, our parents arrived soon after! In two to five minutes, they were there. We screamed for joy! They had a talk with the authorities and minutes later we were on our way home! Somebody say, "never again, never again!"

You see, that is how God is, a very present help in time of trouble. He sees all things, He knows all things and He will show up, right on time.

Almighty Sharing Formula

*That ye may be the children of your Father
who is in Heaven. For He maketh
His sun to rise on the evil and on the good,
and sendeth rain on the just and on the unjust.*
Matthew 5:45

For this story, I will place a disclaimer: I do not remember it, in fact, I choose not to remember it. However, since it was narrated by our "angel of remembrance" (he remembers everything) in the family and confirmed by the others (conspiracy things), there is a 99.9% chance that this happened.

We were in Primary school, and three of us attended holiday lessons. My mum gave us ₦5 for snacks. As the eldest, she gave it to me to hold and share amongst ourselves during the break.

Well, I took ₦4 and gave the other two boys 50 kobo each. Hmm! I am getting old. I actually saw 50 kobo, wow! It is what I call the "Tammy's Almighty Sharing Formula"– ₦2 as my original share; ₦1 for being the eldest; ₦1 for being the only girl. My brothers could share the balance. Come on! this made a lot of sense! Unfortunately, they were not visionary enough to grasp the brilliance of my formula. They were so upset. Of course, I got an ear full when we returned home. For the rest of my life, this story has followed me, and I would not be surprised if my children get to hear it.

That was the end of my sharing role. They never trusted

me to share anything again and would rather give my female cousin who I call my sister. New rules were set such as, if you get to share, you would not pick first, as this typically was done in order of seniority. Smart choice right? Since you did not get to pick first, you had no choice but to do your best to be as impartial as possible. Secondly, once you touched any part, that would be your share, what we called "touch and take". That was necessary as we would sometimes pick up the items to examine and check the size. I must tell you though; my sister is the undisputed champion sharer. She would share items between nine of us and they would all be of equal sizes. Respect!

Thank God that our blessings are not in the hands of any man. You see, if it were up to us, we would be so selfish, blessings would not get around to others. God cares for us all, we must also strive to be like our heavenly Father and treat people equally.

CHAPTER 3

At Thy Right Hand Are Bananas

Thou wilt show me the path of life;
in Thy presence is fullness of joy;
at Thy right hand there are pleasures
for evermore.
Psalm 16:11

My brother will very likely chew me out for putting this story here. Sorry man, I could not resist the temptation!

One of my brothers loves bananas and groundnuts[5] so much. He picked that habit from my dad actually. His favorite type of groundnuts are those still in the pod – boiled or roasted. They are also known in local parlance as "kill and chop", because you have to break (kill) the pods to eat (chop) them. These are so crunchy and even the act of opening each pod to get the groundnut into your hand and then to your mouth is so soothing, almost a flavor on its own. It can be addictive too: once you start breaking those pods, it is difficult to stop until they are all gone.

Flashback! Growing up, we had a dog that died just after it got a new dogshed . As we hoped to get a new dog, we still retained the kennel. After a long while, when this did not happen, we began to store food items in the kennel as it was well built; almost like a mini shed.

On this particular week, it was filled with bananas! This meant nothing to the rest of us, but someone had his eyes set on them. Those bananas were "calling his name" daily and he longed for them. He hatched a plan on how to

---

[5] Also known as peanuts

reach those beautiful ripe bananas and told no one about it.

On this particular day, my mum heard rumblings by her bedroom window, where the shed was situated. It was the sound of joyous crunching! She carefully traced the noise. Sitting on the floor of the shed was this my "banana and groundnut-lover" brother. The stalk of banana and groundnut were on his right side, while the peels were on his left. He had almost gone through one full stalk (not a bunch) of bananas!

It did not matter that he was hunched in a kennel, seated on the floor; all that mattered was that he was having the time of his life. He had unrestricted access to bananas, the love of his life at that time (now his wife and children have taken over in hierarchy; however, bananas and groundnuts are still on his love-list). By the way, he claims groundnut being the love of his life, is fake news! We will settle this in the next family meeting.

There was no other place he wanted to be than with his bananas. God calls us into His presence where there are pleasures for evermore. Like the Psalmist, we must yearn for His presence, *"As the hart panteth after the water brooks, so panteth my soul after thee, O God."* (Psalm 42:1)

Singers on Strike

And whatsoever ye do, do it heartily,
as to the Lord, and not unto men;
Colossians 3:23

The Apostle Numbere dynasty is made up of musicians. We started really early, from when we were children. Leading choirs started early too, as our "child evangel" (Children's Ministry) teachers decided to set up a choir, mirroring the adult church.

My teachers were, Uncle Sabinus, aka Uncle Sabi Sabi; Aunty Mabel, Uncle Alobari and Aunty Stella (Late), God bless you all. I was the honorable, first choir mistress of this choir! *kimon*[6], *flips hair*

We would sing every Sunday before the sermon. Choir practice was during the week, under the mango tree, using a blackboard and chalk. We also had our own band – native drums and instruments. My favorite intro of all time…

Gong (*ke ke ke di ke ke, ke ke di ke ke…*)
Choristers – *gbam, gbam* (feet stomp)
Drums (*ke ke ke ke ke ke……*)
Attend to my prayer so I can know the more…… (singing)

---

[6] Come on!

I can hear members of that choir singing already. Some of the songs were really funny!

Anyway, leadership passed down to my siblings, in order of seniority and the choir just exploded and kept setting the bar higher and higher.

Well, my local church then invested in musical instruments and set up a band. This was very uncommon then so you can imagine the excitement. Even though I was still in children's church, I migrated to their practice! Guess what? I played the keyboard on the Sunday unveiling of this new band! First song - Abraham's blessings are mine! Step aside Divine Basil Frank (Music Producer), before you were, I was!

The point here is that my 'umbilical cord' is buried in the praise/worship ministry. By the grace of God, as a teen, I was among adults and just expressing my gift.

Well, everyone in the music ministry is familiar with its challenges and ups and downs. This particular event had a lasting effect on me.

So, we were in one of those low periods, and my local church choir was invited to minister in the central program. Notice was given one month ahead, but nothing happened – no rehearsals, absolutely no plans.

On the week of the program, "superhero" Tammy stepped in… (Please play the A-Team music here). I spoke with my friend, Grace and I gathered the people, got a song, hired instrumentalists (we did not have) – I went all out. Within four days we were ready, ministered and it was AWESOME! The choir was on fire!!!

A meeting was scheduled the week after. My head was so swollen, *kai!* Today, they will blow my trumpet. 'Tammy saved the day!' So, I and my over-bloated ego arrived at the meeting. Somehow, it started going left, and my ego was slowly sipping out like a balloon deflating. To prompt them, I said "Nobody said thank you to the instrumentalists". *Emmm*[7], silence! Little did I know there was more in store.

Then the killer blow: someone got up and said "Next time, Tammy and Grace should not impose themselves on us. They should have come to tell us first before teaching us a

---

[7] Hum

song or bringing instrumentalists". Yep, that was the "THANK YOU" I was waiting for!

I was completely deflated. All I could feel was hot air rising to my head. *Huh?* I picked my jaw from the floor and went home. *"Chai!* Me? Impose? After all I did? *No wahala*[8]! I will not impose again!" I felt sick in my stomach and I was deeply hurt.

The next day was a rehearsal and I attended. Then the drama began. "Who is going to teach us?" Silence. The person managing the choir that day, went into praise and worship. Oh, we praised the Lord! Intermittently he would ask, "does anyone have something to teach?" Silence. We sang again! This time, he tried to catch my eye. As for me, I refused to volunteer like other times, no, I would not impose again! Men and brethren, we closed choir practice without doing anything that day.

Smiling mischievously to myself, I went home, but the "Good man" was waiting for me.

---

[8] No problem

Good man: You went on strike *nde*[9]? *Ngwanu*[10] clap
for yourself!
Me:(speechless)
Good man: You went on strike for me?
Me: You? *Mbanu*[11], how can? It was for them
Good man: Yes, Me. You did it to me

And I had an ear full of how He can replace me in a heartbeat. All I could say was, "I am sorry, Lord!"

That right there is why I "*carry the matter for head o*" (fully involved)! By the grace of God, I do not need titles to work, it is no longer about you but about Him. Once in a decade, someone manages to cause that level of offense. Do I get hurt? Yes, I do. The worst I can do is take a step back to heal and come right back in. I also do not deliberately seek for accolades.

They are good and should be done to encourage people, but it ceased to be my aim while working for God. All I want as Max Lucado would put it, are the "accolades of

---

[9] Really?
[10] Alright
[11] No way

heaven". Never again, did I hold back my ability just to watch and see the work crumble.

Angelina Ibe, whom we call Aunty Angie, is the oldest serving chorister I know. She is my role model when it comes to staying at your duty post. Since I was a child, Aunty Angie has been in the choir. I grew up, joined her, got married and she is still there. She only stopped very recently due to mobility issues.

If the Lord tarries, that is what I pray to do: serve Him faithfully, till I am old and grey, with my walking stick. I might be croaking (apologies to that generation) but I will be right there, serving with all the strength I can muster. So help me God!

> It pays to serve Jesus, I speak from my heart;
> He'll always be with us, if we do our part;
> There's naught in this wide world can pleasure afford,
> There's peace and contentment in serving the Lord.
>
> I love Him far better than in days of yore,
> I'll serve Him more truly than ever before;

I'll do as He bids me, whatever the cost,
I'll be a true soldier — I'll die at my post.

(Hymn, It pays to serve Jesus by E Il G. Christy)

CHAPTER 5

Before You Call, I Will Answer

And it shall come to pass, that before they call, I will answer; and while they are yet speaking, I will hear.
Isaiah 65:24

Before I got married, I had this little "Tokunbo" (fairly used) Nissan car that I loved so much. I would wash it myself daily. I could handle everything about it except break downs and mechanical issues. As with all "Tokunbo" cars, not everything worked.

One day while driving in Port Harcourt on the popular Rumuola flyover, this my beloved car did not see anywhere else to stop, but right at the top! *See hand falling* (I was embarrassed)!

If you were familiar with this flyover, it was very small and had only one lane on each side. Today, this has changed as it has been expanded. *Chai*[12]! Fine girl like me! I was stuck. So embarrassed, I stepped out of the car. I did not know which was my biggest issue – the fact that I needed to push the car all by myself down the bridge, or the difficulty in getting help at that location, or the traffic I had caused behind me.

Nobody could move. The guy right behind me, jumped out and helped me push it very close to the wall so he

---

[12] Oh dear

could drive past. That worked. Small cars squeezed their way past me, just managing not to scratch my car.

I opened the bonnet, staring at the engine, not knowing what to do! I placed an SOS call home and waited for help. As the cars squeezed by, some driving on the road divider, people just stared at me. Some said, "fine girl, sorry", "*Eyah*[13]".

I do not even remember if I prayed at all, but I sure kept murmuring, "What kind of embarrassment is this?" Guess what? God saw me and my murmuring like He saw Hagar! First, someone I knew showed up. He recognized me while trying to squeeze past. He told me he was coming back as he could not park on the bridge as well. He drove off the bridge, parked safely and walked back towards me on the bridge.

I watched him walk towards me, so happy to have some help, not knowing God was two steps ahead. Suddenly a big lorry carrying people was next to pass. Of course, it was too big to squeeze past. Now there was more build-up.

---

[13] What a pity

There was no way out: he could not go back, and he could not go forward until I was out of the way. Next thing I heard, "*Osho gbe! Osho gbe!*" (chant), all the men in the lorry, about six to ten of them, jumped down. They told me to get in and drive. They began to push the car away and down the bridge.

My friend who had walked up close by this time, jumped in and took over the steering wheel, revving the car and driving to get it started while these men pushed the car.

I just kept smiling as I took a walk down the bridge to catch up with them. The car started and I was able to drive back home. I was amazed at how God could step into any situation and provide solutions.

Well, I learnt a little mechanical work after that. Next time check the battery-head first, it could be disconnected, and you could be driving around with an uncharged battery, which can run down. Thanks for attending my TED talk!

CHAPTER 6

Is It 6 Or 9?

*If it be possible, as much as lieth
in you, live peaceably with all men.
Romans 12:18*

In the year 2003 AD, I, Tammy, served my fatherland. Not like I had a choice though; it is mandatory to spend one year in service to the nation under the National Youth Service Corps scheme (NYSC).

My primary assignment was in one of the paramilitary institutions in Abuja. A conference was held and I was one of the ushers. As part of tourism activities, guests were taken to the foot of Aso Rock (Aso Rock is a large outcrop of granitic rock located on the outskirts of Abuja, the capital of Nigeria[14]), where a little eatery was set up opposite the rock. It had a native theme, and served local delicacies such as *nkwobi*[15], *isi-ewu*[16], *abacha*[17] also known as African salad etc and the main drink was palmwine aka 'palmy'. When we got there, I joined the team serving food.

A lot of people had gathered around the palmy corner. So, I laughed and said, "No driver should take this drink". Palm wine is alcoholic, and I was simply restating the "do not drink and drive" slogan.

Feeling like the official comedian of the day, I strolled past

---

[14]   Source: Wikipedia.org

[15]   Spicy Nigerian dish made with cow foot

[16]   Traditional Nigerian dish made with goat head

[17]   A popular cassava dish native to the Igbos in Eastern Nigeria

thinking to myself, "I probably should start a career in comedy". Everyone laughed at my joke, well, except one person, a driver. By 2003, we had mobile phones, so before we returned to the conference venue, I was in the news.

"Tammy insulted a driver". I was trending, the entire driving pool was furious with me. Our leader who was present said she saw nothing wrong with what I said. Well, they all advised me to apologize to him, as it would cost me nothing.

The next day, I saw him and said, "I am sorry, sir, if you feel I insulted you". He embarrassed me! He screamed, "I have your mate at home, my children are older than you" and other unprintable things at the top of his voice, then he stormed out. All eyes were on me, I was so embarrassed, I started crying.

What did I do wrong? I could not understand it. Since they were driving, they should not drink alcohol. It did not end there. The news kept airing on "radio without battery[18]" – "Tammy insulted a driver". For weeks, some

---

[18] Gossip mill

people, would stop me to ask what happened. Finally, another much older lady, closer to his age, called me into her office, and there he was seated. She asked me to apologize. I said, "I did, and he embarrassed me". She said, "Do it again". I apologized again. This man took off one more time, pouring his anger on me. He spoke of how he would get his children to answer me etc. I stood there listening to him, completely confused at his anger. At some point, the lady told him it was enough. Thankfully, that ended the matter and he accepted my apology.

For years after then, I would tell this story, still very perplexed why this man was upset with me. Not until the year 2008, when I told the story to someone and he said, "Oh my goodness, he understood it as a status thing. He felt you were saying he should not drink because of his status as a driver".

Eureka! I screamed! Finally, the mystery was solved. Now I see why he was so upset, and he had every right to be since that was his understanding. I wished I could find him; I would have apologized over again and explained it was not because of his status but because he could get intoxicated and that would be dangerous since he was driving. I was thankful for one thing, the fact that I apologized and made peace with him even though I did not understand his pain.

Everyone sees things differently. Depending on where you stand, a number could be 9 or it could be 6. Give people the benefit of doubt and do all you can to always be at peace.

CHAPTER 7

Phone A Friend

*A man that hath friends must
shew himself friendly: and there is a
friend that sticketh closer than a brother.*
Proverbs 18:24

While still on NYSC, my pastor and his wife were scheduled to visit my house on a Sunday. I decided to cook for my special guests. I had rice and needed fish but as you can imagine, *"everywhere don red"* (I was so broke). Serving snacks was not an option for me. You see, they were coming from quite a distance and I was not going to serve them biscuits. My mum would always treat every visitor like a king and anyone coming from a distance got proper food. I learnt that from her.

I remembered somewhere fish was sold cheaper but further away from where I lived. I calculated my transport to and fro the shop, the cost of the fish per kilo and my transport to church the next day. Just enough with no extra change. I do not remember the distances, but I can tell you they were far apart. I kept my transport for Sunday at home and went out.

Guess what? Prices had increased, enough to eat up my transport. Dim the lights:

Question No 1:   You do not have enough money for fish and transport. What would you do?

Option A: Go home and do not buy the fish

Option B: Buy the fish, take a cab and pay with the little at home.

Option C: Buy the fish and call a friend.

I sat in front of that shop thinking of my options while the suspense music played in my head. Option A would mean I would not be serving my guests food. Nope, I would not be able to sleep well that night. Option B, there was nothing at home. Since it was not a restaurant, I could not wash plates in lieu. So, nope! Option C: Yes, I had one friend in that city who would get me out of there and back home! I could call him anytime, any day – Teejay!

I took Option C, I bought the fish with all the money on me. Crazy right? To worsen it, my battery was about to die off. I quickly copied his phone number, got to a call center, used the change (one minute only) and called Teejay! "Hey man! I am stranded, come and help me."

Relaxed, I waited, and he showed up. A few minutes later, I could hear my name in the distance "Tammy". Who else but Teejay, driving like crazy to save the day. I later realized he drove with the tank almost empty. Thank God it was enough to take us back to town.

Needless to say, many lessons learned.

God is always available, we can call on Him anytime, any day. I also learned a valuable lesson in friendship, and I pray my friends can rely on me as well such that whenever they think of top five friends who will always be there for them, I should be one.

CHAPTER 8

Peace In The Midst of The Storm

*And, behold, there arose a great tempest
in the sea, insomuch that the ship was covered
with the waves: but he was asleep.
And his disciples came to him, and awoke him,
saying, Lord, save us: we perish. And he saith
unto them, Why are ye fearful, O ye of little faith?
Then he arose, and rebuked the winds and the sea;
and there was a great calm.*
Matthew 8:24 – 26

I come from Buguma, a riverine community in the mangroves of Rivers State, Nigeria. You can imagine the excitement when my dad took us for the first time to see our hometown, popularly called Buguma City. We had fun visiting Mary Wood College, which was situated away from the village and you had to walk across a wooden bridge over the river. We enjoyed it so much that once we had a house built, visits became an annual event every Christmas. We would go into the swamp to pick periwinkles, swim in brackish water and catch *ikoli* (crabs). This was our Bahamas!

There were no roads then to Buguma; we went by speed boat from the popular Abonnema Wharf, Port Harcourt. Our home was open to all, so at least twenty or more people would make the trip, and we would need two speed boats to take the entire family. If you have ever been on a boat, you know the waves increase once another boat is on the path and in the opposite direction. We looked forward to these moments. As the wave would hit the boat it would bounce on the waves, lifting everyone in the boat slightly up. Screams of delight - "*eh, eh, eh….*" would rent the air. Oh, I love boat rides.

I had to give this background to let you know I enjoy the

sea. Well, I thought I did until I crossed the famous Bonny bar! Bonny is one of the islands in Rivers State, but on the Atlantic Ocean. Its reputation precedes it – the waves are out of this world.

In 2005, I got an opportunity to work in a company on Bonny Island. The plan was to go over, fill out paperwork and then come back to Port Harcourt, get my things and return to resume work.

My dad was traveling to visit the Church there, so he took me along. He hired a bigger boat than the open speed boat I was used to. It even had a cover, so we did not see much of the sea. We got in, I took my seat, relaxed and off we went. As we navigated the creeks, I just kept saying, "Is this the Bonny Bar people are afraid of? There is nothing to be afraid of". Little did I know that the waves at Bonny Bar were watching me in 3D.

Well, it was time to cross the bar! Then I saw the true definition of waves. Boy! As the waves hit the boat, we would fly up and then bounce back on the sea with such ferocity, my heart was popping out of my mouth and I was sweating profusely.

Only for me to take a look at my dad, he was watching me, and smiling. The man did not even shake. I was like…. "Whatttt? Are we in the same boat or not?" Wow! Such peace in the midst of the storm. He had this assurance that nothing was going to happen (of course) but most importantly, he was actually enjoying the storm. I sure felt like those disciples. We arrived safely but not before my spirit had left my body several times! *Phew!*

You see all those grand plans of doing paperwork and returning to Port Harcourt to pack my stuff? All up in the air! I was so shaken I refused to step off that island. My things were sent to me via boat and I kept my feet firmly on the ground until the job was over about four to five months later. Now it was time to exit! I told my parents, "*gbala gbala*[19]", so they got me booked on a much biggerrrr boat (hovercraft) and I returned home. Men and brethren, I have not stepped foot in Bonny after that. Hopefully, we get a road soon. Until then!

When storms of life come, that is the attitude God wants us to have - assurance, peace, actually a smile or even laughter! Enjoy the ride; the Master is in your boat. There is only one outcome, arriving safely at the shore!

---

[19] Never, never

CHAPTER 

Deliver Us from Evil

One of the few down-sides of our Christmas Holiday in Buguma was that we had to go into the town to fetch water in jerry cans, as our house was out on the sand-filled area. Of course, as kids, we did not particularly mind.

However, we noticed a lady was always following us. She had this eerie smile, would not say a word but just followed behind. We believed she was a mad woman. Once we sighted her we would start running. The more we ran, the more she followed. One of those days, it appeared she was determined to catch up with us. We ran towards our house and she followed! We screamed and at some point, since we could not run fast enough, we abandoned our water cans and ran "for our lives".

That night, we called for an emergency conference of all the children in the house. The conference began. What do we do about this mad woman who keeps chasing us? We cannot keep running forever. Someone suggested that there is a saying that if you flogged a mad person, they would stop chasing you. Another said it was sand we needed to pour on her. Well, it was settled. We were going to flog her the next time she came towards us; no more running. We armed ourselves with sticks, canes, name it, in preparation for the next encounter.

The next day, my parents were sitting outside in the evening, enjoying the smell of the mangrove and the cool wind when we saw this lady heading towards them. Noise! Rumbling amongst the children. We passed the message on, "Charly to Bravo, target sighted, over!"

Well, she walked up to them, and they gave her a seat. *Hmm!* Next thing we heard, "Tammy, Wari, Orinaba..." it was my dad's voice, calling for all of us. We ran and assembled at the muster point. Close up, she did not look mad at all. He looked at us and said, pointing to the lady seated beside him, "This is my sister (relative), she says you run when she tries to talk with you." Silence! He told us to stop running and asked us to greet her properly. We did and ran off.

All we could think about was all the plans we had for her, the sticks we had gathered to give her a thorough beating. Oh my goodness! God saved her... *ahhh!* No, actually, God saved us! Imagine if we had carried out our plans.... *Ewo*[20]! * hands on the head*.

---

[19] Oh no!

CHAPTER 10

Under the Shadow of Your Wings

He who dwells in the secret place of the Most High Shall abide under the shadow of the Almighty. I will say of the LORD, "He is my refuge and my fortress; My God, in Him I will trust." Surely He shall deliver you from the snare of the fowler and from the perilous pestilence. He shall cover you with His feathers, And under His wings you shall take refuge;
Psalm 91:1 – 4

I have seen this Scripture fulfilled in my life several times but will only recount two of those incidents – where God delivered me from a road accident, and from armed robbers.

One of the commercial markets located in Eastern Nigeria is the Ariaria Market in Aba, Abia State. Traders from Port Harcourt usually go to this market to buy things at wholesale price for resale in town at a markup. Thus, if you wanted to save some money, you would head to Ariaria Market just like the traders to get cheaper rates.

On this particular day in 2003, I had gone to the Ariaria market in the company of a guardian and the driver who took us with a bus. I was serving my country (NYSC) at the time and went shopping in preparation to return to Abuja, where I was posted to. Once we were done shopping, we headed back to Port Harcourt. My guardian had dropped off at Aba, as she had other things to do in the city. The road typically has heavy traffic as it connects Rivers State to Abia State and is also a common route for traders. At the time, one side was under construction, so drivers from both sides made use of just one lane.

Along the journey, I decided to lay down on the back seat

and take a quick nap. Pardon me, at the time, I knew nothing about safety. Not long after, I heard the driver screaming, "JESUS! JESUS!! JESUS!!!". He revved the engine and accelerated, screaming all the while. I tried to get up, but I was thrown back as the bus jerked. I could hear screams from outside and then a loud screeching sound. I knew we were in trouble, even though I could not see, so I joined him to call on the Lord, "JESUS! JESUS!! JESUS!!!".

Gradually, the driver was able to bring the bus to a stop by the side of the road and both of us jumped out. He was in so much shock, he sat by the road. I was shaken also but not as badly as him. Cars parked by and people trooped out to make sure we were okay.

Here's what happened. The driver while trying to overtake a vehicle in front, had miscalculated the distance of the vehicle coming in the opposite direction. Guess what? It was a heavy-duty trailer. We were about to have a head-on collision with a trailer. God was so merciful.

After putting myself together, I took a walk around the bus to ascertain the damage to the bus. The trailer missed us by a split hair. We literally squeezed through and the side of the bus took the hit.

How we survived could only have been God. What was even more interesting was that He spared me the trauma of seeing the accident: I had just laid down when it happened. The damage was so serious, we had to call home for someone to come pick us up, and the bus had to be towed into town on another day.

Another incident occurred one of those times I was on the road en route to Abuja to continue with my Youth Service. There were five of us in the car, including the driver. As we approached Lokoja, Kogi State, we slowed down for what we thought was Police carrying out routine checks on the road, since there were cars lined up ahead of us. Alas! They were armed robbers. Yep! In the middle of the day! Apparently, they had already robbed three cars in front of us.

My heart skipped. I screamed, "JESUS! JESUS!! JESUS!!!". Instinctively, I shut my eyes tight, raised my hands, and my mobile phone slipped to the floor of the car. They ordered us to come out and lay on the floor, and then patted us down, collecting cell phones and a handbag.

Suddenly, we heard the patter of footsteps and then silence. Of course, my eyes were tightly shut, in fact if I could close them further, I would have. What we heard next was a male voice, "Get up, get up and go!"

It was the Police: they arrived just in time before the armed robbers could do a proper raid of our vehicle and properties. The armed robbers saw them and ran into the bush. We got into our car and zoomed off. My phone was still in the car, and my luggage intact. Praise God!

Thanks be to God Who guides, protects and delivers us from trouble.

CHAPTER 11

Wait, I Say on the Lord

*Wait on the LORD: be of good courage,
and he shall strengthen thine heart:
wait, I say, on the LORD.*
Psalm 27:14

I graduated from the University in the year 2002, did my compulsory paramilitary service to the nation (Youth service) at Abuja in 2003, spent an extra year working in 2004 and returned home early 2005. I expected a job immediately after service and had my eyes on the industry I wanted to work for. My plan staying back in 2004 was that as soon as I got a job, I would return home, but one year passed and nothing happened.

This should not have been a problem, I graduated with a Second-class upper division (2.1) and my dad is Apostle Numbere. He *"carried my matter on his head"* that is, he practically went job hunting for me (love you dad), but nothing happened. I really could not understand why. Feeling really low, I came back home, my parents encouraged me to enroll in a master's degree program.

This was now 2006. I remember in one of the Healing Services (a special church service held once a month), Jubilee Voices (my choir) sang "Restoring the Years" by Donald Lawrence. I cried my eyes out: "Lord, remember me! I need a job." Soon after that, my pastor (once my pastor, always my pastor, *wink*), Pastor Ibim Alabraba was preaching on Psalm 27:14. I can still hear him shouting, "Wait, I say on the Lord! Wait for Him, He is coming! Wait for Him, He is coming". Any time I read that verse, I still hear his voice.

And yes, God arrived. What did He do? He addressed my IGNORANCE first!

My favorite cousin back then (he has since lost his position), Ifeanyi Katchy nicknamed Boy G (Boy Genius) by the Numbere clan, visited.

Boy G: "Young lady, why don't you have a job yet?"
Me: "I do not know, nobody has employed me."
Boy G: "Have you submitted your CV (Curriculum Vitae) at any bank?"
Me: "*Emm…*no!"
Boy G: "Have you submitted your CV to any company?"
Me: "*Emm…* no!"
By this time, I was scratching my head. He laughed, "*Ó ò serious*[21]". "How do you want to get a job then?"

You see, I was waiting for a miracle but wanted it to fall from the sky! How was God going to give me a job when nobody had my CV in the first place? *Ahh*, scales fell from my eyes!

---

[21] You are not serious

We got on the internet and he showed me that all companies have a "careers" session on their websites. We went through major ones and I submitted unsolicited applications. We set out a plan for me to go around submitting copies of my CV, to banks and other institutions around.

Guess what? One of them was going through a recruitment process. Within two weeks, I got invited for a test. I passed, did the interview and in a space of four months from when God told me He was coming, I was employed. One of the ones my dad was pursuing also came through within this period, but I ran away! I have been working there for fourteen years as at the time of writing! Glory to God!

Today, there is so much information out there about school, jobs, business etc, yet I have met people who do not know what a Curriculum Vitae (CV) is; who do not know how to write one; and who drop out of school programs and trainings. Not acceptable!

Get informed, do your part and trust God to open doors and do the rest. I say to you, "Wait on the Lord, He is coming!"

CHAPTER 12

Stranger Than Fiction

*Are not two sparrows sold for a farthing? and one
of them shall not fall on the ground without your
Father. But the very hairs of your head are all
numbered. Fear ye not therefore, ye are of more
value than many sparrows.*
Matthew 10:29 - 31 ; Matthew 6:25 -34

This story is a bit embarrassing, but once in a while, I get the courage to share! Now I am putting it in print (I hope I do not regret this).

We got the job, yeah! *fist pump* and I got the opportunity to travel for my first training overseas. All was good until one of the days, they told us we would go for Go-karting the next day as a team building event (Google isyour friend).

My friends helped me out with sports gear, but it was dreadfully small. I squeezed myself in and guess what? *Creeeeek*! Every step I took, I could hear that sound. No, not the sound of rain, but the sound of a tear. *Ahhh*! Trouble! *hands on my head*

You see, I am a very shy person (Stop laughing! I can hear you.) For real, I am still very shy. I would rather endure the situation and find a way to adjust before I raise my hand in a crowd. I could not tell anyone. The right thing to do was to excuse myself, right? But no, full blown adult like Tammy was too shy to talk *facepalm*.

Well, we lined up at the centre in teams ready to go into the go-kart. Excitement everywhere but I was about to pass out. I knew that the moment I stepped in, the last piece of cloth that covered my decency would be gone and in public o! My bride price was about to be reduced! *Mogbe*[22]!

But you see this God, He cares about EVERYTHING about us. Nothing is too small, and nothing is too big. Those thoughts that cannot be said, He hears. Those words that are too embarrassing to be uttered, He knows. What happened next, still gives me chills even as I write this.

Two or three people away from my turn, suddenly, the sky cracked open. There was thunder, lightning and heavy downpour. Immediately, someone came out and started handing out full-size raincoats to everyone.

See, I jumped into God's arms and gave Him a big hug, literally. Tears of joy! I took mine and it covered me completely. I had real fun, my heart was full of joy, gratitude and humility at the greatness of God.

---

[21] I am in trouble

HE SEES me, HE was right there with me. He knew my weakness and He took care of me in a way I would never have imagined. I LOVE YOU, JESUS!

Someone might say it was a coincidence, but as far as I am concerned, that was my God, right there and in the nick of time.

His eye is on the sparrow, I KNOW He watches me!

See, we have God, why should we worry? He wants us to talk to Him about anything and absolutely everything. He is interested in EVERYTHING about us and He is able to take care of us.

Wings of A Dove

---

*And I said, Oh that I had wings
like a dove! for then would I fly away,
and be at rest.
Psalm 55:6*

So, I returned, fired up, ready to work! You know this picture you have in your head about work! Boss Lady – suit, high heels, bounce in and out of the office, speaking *funee*[23], you can even hear the music play in your head!

In a few weeks, the euphoria was over, I was down from cloud nine, face first. Work is WORK!

Ọmọ[24], it was not easy! I was confused, dazed! Too many feelings! I did not know *"jack"* (anything), I kept making mistakes up and down. You see that shyness? Ah, it was in its full glory. I would wake up in the morning CRYING! Real tears! "I do not want to go to work! I do not want to go to work!" As I stepped into the office, my heart would race frantically, I would count the minutes until the day was over. In fact, I was the alarm clock to tell everyone it was time to go home. I would literally run away. God bless you, my husband! His work was to wipe my tears away.

During my interview, I had mentioned "Ability to work under pressure" as one of my strengths. My recruiter, Femi Adewumi of blessed memory, laughed and said, "No, you do

---

[23] Foreign accent
[24] Boy! (Exclamation)

not know what that is!" He was right. It was so much, I would sleep-talk, "Finder, model" etc. My husband, poor guy, he said he did not know what they had done to his wife.

In short, I wanted out and fast! I called my parents up. I lamented, I wanted to resign. I just wanted to drop my papers. I told them I was ready to work in Dad's office. "I beg to apply" did not include this kind of work. They calmed me down and offered the solution they know is the only solution – they told me they would pray! And pray, they did! (thank you, dad and mum, you're the best!)

One Sunday, Dr. C. S. Ejimadu (my brother-in-law) was the preacher. One verse: Psalm 55:6. If I had wings I would fly away. He described vividly how situations make us wish we had wings to fly away and escape. We just want "OUT". He said, no, that could be exactly where God wants you to be. His message was not that God will bring you out NOW; It was "Go through the process!"

Looking back, I see God was working. First, I found favor. One of my clients treated me like his daughter, he covered me and was patient through my learning curve. I am forever grateful. I had a support system, my family, my friends who I call my sisters, Ego, Erebi, Mama Comfort Udoh (she was my escape).

What would I tell my younger self today? Go through the process. There is a time for sowing and a time for reaping, learn, put your back to work, put the effort in and God will do the rest. Get mentors, people who will help you navigate the new environment.

Flying or running away is and never has been a solution! I love the quote: "The will of God will never lead you where the grace of God cannot keep you."

Did everything go smoothly after then? *Lai lai*[25]! Next story!

---

[25] Not true

CHAPTER 14

Breaking of Day

For his anger endureth but a moment;
in his favour is life: weeping may endure
for a night, but joy cometh in the morning.
Psalm 30:5

I wish I could tell you the tables turned immediately. Nope! That is not how it worked for me! But, I was no longer agitated. The tears stopped while I waited for "the consolation of Israel".

Seven years after, events swung from very bad, to bad, to not so bad, then okay and back again to very bad. I became somewhat a disgruntled employee. Sometimes I was angry, sometimes sad, other times passive and sometimes bland. So far, it was the worst period of my career.

Then at a point when I thought I was going to have some form of stability, the carpet was swept off my feet – the project I was on ended. Now I had something else to worry about – job security. Back at the base, I knew I was idle; I was doing nothing. No employer allows that. I was super worried. I would resume in the morning and if I was truthful to myself, I felt idle and useless. Oh, how I wanted more.

One of those days I was driving to work. I still remember I was at Old Aba road, Port Harcourt, driving towards new Aba Road, Port Harcourt. I began talking to God. My heart was full. I cried out! You know when you start talking to yourself, people *go think say you don kolo* (people think you are mad).

Dear God, "You promised me everything would be alright. Where is everything you promised?"

Well, He answered with that Scripture: "Weeping may endure for a night, joy will come in the morning". Basically, He said that the day breaks just at the darkest hour. I was feeling so overwhelmed because I had reached the darkest hour and at that point, the day was about to break! Glory to God!

As soon as I got to the office, I started writing the song "Breaking of Day". Sent it to my brother, James and he got inspired immediately and put a beautiful tune to the words.
Here are the lyrics:

Solo 1: You have believed God's word
  And you have claimed His promises
  That your deliverance is here
  And your healing is now
  You watch and wait and pray
  As time goes by you ask
  Where is my miracle?
  Where is my promise?
  But this can only mean something's about to begin
  Cos at the darkest hour, the morning will come

Chorus: (Hold on) I can see the dawn of day
(Hold on) dark night's gonna pass away
(Hold on) it is gonna be a brighter day
Stand strong, don't be weary
(Hold on) I can see your breakthrough come
(Hold on) the sun is gonna rise again
Cos at the end you'll see
The breaking of day

Solo 2: I've reached the darkest point
There's no more strength to wait
My faith is fading and my heart is breaking
My burden's so heavy
I've got to ask right now
Where is my miracle?
Where is my promise?
But this can only mean something's about to begin
Cos at the darkest hour, the morning will come

Bridge: But you say "I've been waiting too long,
I believe my time is past"
Hold on, be strong
There's no time with God
He will come through
Hold on

Refrain: Rising Up
    The sun is rising up
    Passing by
    The night is passing by
    (I can see)

Oh yes, the day broke forth!

What I thought was the end of a job, was divine displacement to position me properly. I was at the right place at the right time and guess what? Things took a drastic positive turn from that moment. The sun rose again. God put in place managers who were nothing short of angels, who saw my potential that I did not see and took a chance on me (I would not call their names for security reasons). I learnt that "Every exit door is the entry door to another place"

I became HAPPY! Yes, you can be happy in your workplace. That same place of "sorrow" became a place of "joy". Of course, no life is perfect. I still have challenges here and there, but I face them and see them as springboards to greater heights. More importantly, I am happy.

What would I tell my younger self today? There are lessons to learn in EVERY SITUATION. Learn them and GROW! Mentors, mentors, mentors! You need them. Whatsoever your hands find to do, do it with all your heart. Do it as unto God and not to man. Do it for yourself! God will be there to see you through!

CHAPTER 15

My Thoughts Towards You

For my thoughts are not your thoughts,
neither are your ways my ways,
saith the LORD.
Isaiah 55:8

So, things picked up at work. I was happy and enjoying my new responsibilities when things changed suddenly and put me on a new trajectory.

Prior to this time, I was in the technical domain and I knew someone that always teased me, "I will tell your boss to put you in Sales". I would shrug my shoulders, "No way, if you put me in Sales, I will resign". I hated it, literally. He kept saying this, and my answer was the same, "I will resign". Well, he was prophesying and did not know it.

You see, the Sales role involved a lot of face-time and interactions with clients. There's no hiding behind a computer or telephone, human interaction, engagement and relationship are key. For a shy person like myself (yes, I said that again), that was asking for too much. Well, I am shy until you give me a microphone! *HOYA*[26]!

Fast forward to some years later and there was an opening for a sales role. *Wetin concern me?* (what's my business?). Well, God had other plans.

---

[26] Chant

The wonderful people who were in management at that time, decided I would take up the role. My sister, Ego was the one to deliver the news. She bounced into my office with her "one and half" leg (inside joke) and said, "Madam, you are taking up this role" and bounced out the way she came. I looked at her in disbelief, watched her walk away and managed to close my mouth, right on time before a fly got in. She did not even give me an option.

I asked some questions to clarify my concerns and with the encouragement of my family and friends, I took up the role. I did have teething problems when I asked myself, "what have you done?", but once that phase was over, I must tell you; it has been great. It is everything I wanted but did not know I wanted it.

Wait, did I say I would resign? Me? Are you sure I am the same person?

What did I learn? God has plans for me that are bigger and better than mine. I could not even think up such a fantastic plan even if I tried. I have learned to trust and obey Him.

God is the only Perfection

In all thy ways acknowledge him,
and he shall direct thy paths.
Proverbs 3:6

Work continued and I was flying. In my mind, I became so confident in my job that if I am truthful to myself, I actually tilted over the edge. I was no longer dependent on God, who I always drew strength from. Somehow, I began to give Him the back seat. I felt like a "superstar", you know!

Well, He jolted me back to reality. One of those weeks, everything that could have gone wrong, went wrong. I was making rookie mistakes and struggling with tasks that were normally a walkover. I was even shocked at myself. I was more disappointed in myself than even my management was.

I apologized profusely. How would I get out of this mess? Mails were flying, some were hard and rightfully so. Just to mention that by this time, after my "Breaking of day", I had fantastic bosses back to back. The one in charge at the time of this incidence chatted me up on the messaging tool – "Hi, Tammy". My heart skipped. I was expecting the hammer. What came next was the message below:

"Sometimes God reminds us that we are not in charge of everything and that He is. So, things that should not go wrong will go wrong and it humanizes us, reminds us that He is the only perfection. Do not stress it at all. Smile when you see him 'show Himself'."

I burst out in tears. I closed my office door and cried. Yes, that was exactly what happened. I cried for two reasons. First, nothing evokes repentance like mercy released in the place of judgement that is deserved. I had earned every scolding and was expecting one, but rather, it was an encouragement I got.

Secondly, the reminder was loud, I am nothing without God. I spoke to God, crawled back with my tail in between my legs and just *jejely*[27] placed myself back in His hands.

He took over and matters were resolved.

---

[27] Quietly

As The Deer Panteth
For The Waters

As the hart panteth after the water brooks,
so panteth my soul after thee, O God.
Psalm 42:1

My first child, Chibuisi, is the first grandchild of the Apostle Numbere dynasty. All his grandparents were at the hospital on the day of his arrival: my dad, mum and mother-in-law. He brought so much joy. You know parents become totally new people once they attain the status of grandparents.

My son had a special bond with all his grandparents but was extremely close to his grandpa. He was named Tamuno-Tari[28] by his grandpa and my husband translated that to Ikwerre - Chibuisi. So, he answers both names.

As an infant, he could be crying, all the women in the house would try to no avail to pacify him; but his grandpa would pick him up and rock him to sleep, singing a Kalabari lullaby: *"Ine bo saki, Indo do, da bo saki i ōkōkō peyi; inam/Tari digi a doki do"*. Google cannot help you this time so let me help you. It means, your mother will breastfeed you when she comes, and your dad will give you fish head (some say chicken) to eat when he comes.

My dad said Tari was his, I should go get mine. Literally, he was. By the time he was one, he would cry just to stay at

---

[28] God first

his grandparents' place. So, keeping him overnight became a regular feature. It graduated from one night to several nights in some cases.

One of those days, I said, "This is my son, I carried him for nine months. He must come home with me. *Haba*[30]! How can he keep picking his grandparents over me? Today, he is going home with me *by fire, by force*[31]*!*"

I bundled him into the car and strapped him in his car seat, gave him toys and biscuits to keep him busy, wound up the car windows, put on the AC and increased the sound of my radio. That way, if he cried, people on the road would not hear and think I had kidnapped him. *Them think say them stubborn, I will show them say I stubborn pass* (I will have my way).

His grandparents were sitting outside. They said their goodbyes and I drove off, determined to get home with my son.

Then the drama began. Do you know wailing?

---

[30] What
[31] By all means necessary

NOTHING could pacify him. The more he wailed, the more I drove off *(Today na today[32]!)*. He screamed, "grandpa, grandma". He wailed! Cried his eyes out! Well, I could not keep up, my heart broke. I was almost crying with him. I could not take it anymore. By this time, I had driven quite a distance, but I reversed and drove all the way, back to my parents.

They were still at the spot where I left them. I got him out of the car into the arms of his grandpa. They were both screaming. "What did you do to my grandson? Give me my child!" He just crumbled into his grandpa's arms while he wiped his tears away.

I drove back to the waiting arms of my husband *jọ*, thinking about the petrol I just wasted in my attempt to yank him off his beloved grandparents.

May my heart pant so much for You, Lord that nothing and nowhere else makes sense.

---

[32] It will be settled today

CHAPTER 18

Thoughts of Peace

---

*For I know the thoughts that I think
toward you, saith the LORD, thoughts of peace,
and not of evil, to give you an expected end.
Jeremiah 21:11*

I had my first child, Chibuisi soon after I got married. Everything was perfect. As he approached two years, I was ready for the next baby. Guess what? No show. I was actively trying for another baby, and he or she was not forthcoming. By the third year, I was worried. Anxiety had set in – there was definitely a problem.

I became so anxious. My web searches were "how to get pregnant", "early signs of pregnancy", "signs of ovulation" etc. Between each circle I would count and even miscount, then assume pregnancy until I would get the flow. Oh, the disappointment! The fear!

That period seemed to be a very fertile period around me. Everyone in church seemed to be getting pregnant. I would see pregnant ladies and tears would well up in my eyes.

My husband bore the brunt of my swinging emotions. Some days it was tears, sometimes anger. I told him he did not understand. Mind you, I already had one child. I tried to console myself with that, but nothing could fill that yearning in my heart.

We prayed and God heard. The first thing He did was to

give me peace in my mind. I had so much peace, that the desperation ceased. It was like I forgot about my desire. The moment I stopped worrying, He intervened; with a problem that is. We had an early service in church at 6 AM which was a one-hour service during the week. I remember singing:

What the Lord has done for me, I cannot tell it all (3x)
He saved me and washed me in His blood
So I can shout Hallelujah (2x) I can shout praise the Lord.

The sermon was about thanksgiving. I started experiencing severe stomach pains, but I still went to work afterward. The pain only increased by the day. The summary is that I ended up in the hospital for emergency surgery to get out an inflamed ovary, leaving me with one ovary. The inflamed ovary was the hindrance!

Guess what? The anxiety returned, "How will I have children with just one ovary?", I asked myself. The doctor had said it was okay but his words did not allay my fears. Well, God showed up again; speaking to me in interesting ways: Unsolicited, I kept on stumbling on stories of women who were still able to have babies despite one complication or the other. Then, during one of the church services, my husband preached about Elijah and the cloud like a man's hand. That peace that passes all understanding returned to my heart, and no sooner had the desperation ceased than my first daughter was conceived.

I understood just a little bit what some women go through. I even had one child already while some have none at all. You see, that pain in your heart, sometimes too deep to even share with your husband; the tears in the closet, where you hide to cry so people do not think you are faithless. God sees it all and I pray He will give you peace that passes all understanding.

Thy Will Be Done

*Thy kingdom come. Thy will be done
in earth, as it is in heaven.
Matthew 6:10*

September 2017 was the 45th Anniversary of my church. So excited about the celebration, I actively participated in all events including the rally even though it was pouring. We went around the streets, singing and dancing. I never knew there were "three of us" participating in the rally. Well, the next day, I landed in the emergency ward with severe pains in my abdomen and fever. I could barely walk into the hospital. After an abdominal scan they continued treatment.

A week after, another scan and voilà! two babies! I was dazed, confused, I did not know how to react. I love twins so much, mind you. My husband and I prayed and just thanked God for everything. My husband had some premonition that we were going to lose them, so we prayed that God's will be done.

One week after, I was bleeding profusely. From the scan, one sac was collapsing in an apparent abortion. I was put on medication immediately. I was worried, as I did not want my children to come into this world and suffer from one complication or the other.

We prayed again, LET THY WILL BE DONE! You see this prayer? I think sometimes God just looks at us and asks if we really want His will to be done. At this point, I had conditioned my mind that I was going to lose the babies but still went through with the doctor's recommendation. I braced myself for the worst.

Well, we got an all clear. The twins were doing well and we began to plan for their arrival. *"Mama Ejima"* (mother of twins) loading!*flips hair*.

Fast forward to December at 20 weeks, I woke up and my water broke. I screamed, "Hospital". We rushed down. As soon as I got into the doctor's office, another big gush. I screamed and cried. My babies were leaving. I was put on bed rest but the doctors told me the chances of them surviving was almost zero. They expected the fetus in the ruptured sac to be expelled out of the womb and the other to follow subsequently. After three days in the hospital, I was wheeled into the labour ward to be induced. We were going to lose both of them. I kept asking "Not even one?"

My husband remembered immediately that we had prayed "LET THY WILL BE DONE".

I want to really appreciate my husband, my family, my inlaws, our doctors, loved ones and friends who showed up in the labour ward or called. They arrived at the hospital as soon as they got the information, and some stayed for so many hours to make sure I was alright. I saw each of them and gained strength. They all said the same thing, "We want you alive".

The journey began in the morning and was over at about 10PM. The little girl came out first and took just one breath, too small to survive. The boy was more stubborn though, and the doctors had to battle to get him out. Then the placenta refused to come out... PAIN, TOO MUCH PAIN... physical and emotional!

I cried, oh, I cried till I could hear my heart in my ears. Then I would stop abruptly because I could hear me telling myself, "Tammy, your heart is about to burst". As I began to lactate and had no babies to nurse, all I could remember was *"Rachel weeping for her children, and would not be comforted, because they are not."*(Matthew 2:18). I would raise my hand calling on God to grab that hand literally and pull me out of the black hole of depression that was trying to suck me in. Anyway, people would walk into the room, I would put on a smile but take off the charade when they were gone. As I walked out of the hospital after my discharge, feeling the emptiness in my stomach, I remembered how I walked into the hospital a few days back with my stomach big with my babies. My legs became heavy, I felt like dropping to the floor and having a good cry in public. I said to myself, "so you are leaving here with nothing?" The Comforter told me, "No, you are leaving here with your life". It was like a soothing balm! Indeed, there is a Balm in Gilead.

Well, His will had been executed. Who knows if I could have died? Who knows if the children might have suffered? Who knows what the end would have been? Today, no regrets, I rest in His love and I know He would never have put more on me than I could bear.

The journey to healing was not easy, it took time, but I just trusted God. My family would ask me "How are you doing?", I would say "I am trying". I almost died a month later from high blood pressure but the Almighty God came through.

Songs that kept me going
* Even if by Mercy Me
* You are my strength performed by Maranda Curtis
* He leadeth me (Hymn)
* You are God by Nathaniel Bassey

Next time you pray "LET THY WILL BE DONE", be ready for His will. It might not come in the package you expect, but it is ALWAYS GOOD!

I do not know what your situation is, but if I came out strong and victorious, you too can! *hugs and kisses*.

CHAPTER 20

All Things Work Together For Good

*And we know that all things work
together for good to them that love God,
to them who are the called according to his purpose.*
Romans 8:28

A few weeks after the loss, my blood pressure hit the roof and I did not even realize it. Well, it must have been a proof of the trauma, but that is not the story. The story is about how it was discovered.

My blood pressure was still being monitored, a few spikes here and there but nothing to worry about. I traveled out of my State to see if I could take my mind off things a bit. I never knew there was trouble. You see, hypertension is a silent killer, do not joke with it.

I had excruciating stomach pains that I tried to endure throughout the day to no avail. I could not understand it. The pains increased until around 3AM when I could not bear it anymore so I got a car and went to the hospital. As soon as I stepped into the doctor's office, the pains stopped. I kid you not! We ran several tests and scans and it was clear that there was nothing wrong within my body, it was simply readjusting.

The issue was that my blood pressure was 190/103. That is not a typo! They checked it multiple times; different people with different devices but each time, it went higher. The treatment began immediately. My friend did not let me out of her sight for one minute after this news.

That stomach pain saved my life!

I already explained that in 2010 when my second child was delayed (three years after the first), when God intervened, He did with a problem: Excruciating stomach pain (*hmm*, this is becoming a sign now), which got me in the hospital for emergency surgery to get out an inflamed ovary.

ALL things work together for good! ALL - including problems, will work in harmony for good. Next time that problem shows up, fret not, it will work together for good. Next time that problem shows up, it just might be that, that problem is the solution!

Ah ah... warning: To those who LOVE God!

Loose Lips

A man hath joy by the answer of his mouth:
and a word spoken in due season,
how good is it!
Proverbs 15:23

God came through and I did not lose my life during the loss of the twins or when my blood pressure shot up. Thanks be to God. I was still battling with depressing thoughts but was fighting with all the little strength I could muster. I had a huge support system: my family, friends, the brethren in Church. They rallied around me. However, a few really did not know what to say.

A month after, I decided to get right back into the service of God. I was not going to stay down. I was pumped up. I went for choir practice on Saturday so I could join in the ministration that Sunday. Well, by this time I was what we call "*orobo*[32]"; literally four times my weight. Forget the scale, in my mind, I was a size 12! Of course, my clothes did not fit. I opted to borrow my husband's shirt. He is 6.2 ft tall and I am 5.05ft, so you can imagine how big I had become. Uniform sorted out, I looked forward to that Sunday.

The day arrived, the day I would defy the devil. I would lift my hands and worship just like David did. We arrived and I could already feel the bounce in my feet. Come on! David got nothing on me! Well, more like feel the roll in

---

[32] Overweight

my feet. I was "rolling" literally.

I passed by a few people, some waved, "Good morning Tammy". I waved back, just happy to be alive. The next person stopped me, and we greeted. I never imagined what happened next. "Ah, you have added weight o!" *Huh?* *mouth wide open*. I smiled, said nothing and walked past. If only he/she knew the hell I had been through. Another: "This fat is not good o, you need to do something", then another, "Welcome, but you are now fat." Tears welled up in my eyes. I rolled away, as fast I could, found a quiet place and just let the tears pour. I wiped my tears and then went about my duties in church.

A few hours later and service was over, then it started again. *Kai*[34], the devil planned for me. He had lost the physical battle but the emotional one still raged. Well, one person was the scapegoat. As soon as I heard, "fat" coming out of her mouth, I just blurted out "I just lost my children". It was like a lightning bolt. I walked away while she tried to apologize.

I remember how some people told me it was my fault I lost

---

[34] Oh no!

the babies, literally. "Ah, sorry o, I heard what happened. How come?" I started narrating the story, thinking I had a sympathetic ear (also because sometimes I wanted to talk to ease off the stress). Response? "It was your mind, you did not accept them that is why you lost them" Another, "It was the jumping you were doing". I did not really jump you know, just that I was always active while pregnant. These are not hearsay, they told me to my face. Honestly, I had already given some a big knock on their heads in my mind.

Do I blame them? Not at all! They genuinely did not realize what they were doing and the effect it had on me. We just need to be careful with what we say and how we say what we say. You never know people's struggles. That smile could just be a smokescreen; let your words not cause more pain.

CHAPTER 22

Jonah In The Belly
Of The Plane

And forgive us our trespasses,
as we forgive them that trespass against us.
Matthew 6:12

I have four fantastic brothers and I love them to bits (I can hear them say *Meowww*! Inside joke). You know ministers' children like us are always filled with the Spirit of God, tongues talking, demon binding etc. We do not have disagreements at all. Yeah right! Welcome to the real world. We have at one point or the other caused each other pain and been the source of hurt.

One of those days, I was at the receiving end and one of them upset me so badly, we had a huge disagreement. I will let you guess which of them. I was so hurt and pained to the point I made some scary decisions.

One: this was the last straw. Two: I would not forget this one. Three: I would cut off and not allow any familiarization. Going forward, our relationship would be strictly formal.

I was traveling and got on a flight and my conversation with the "Good man" and the "bad man" began!

Bad man: "Every time they treat you like a doormat."
Me: "*Eh hen*[35]!"

---

[35] Yes

Bad man: "Remember you are the eldest."

Me: "That is right."

Bad man: "Enough is Enough! No going back on this!"

Me: "Exactly!"

Good man: "But you must forgive."

Bad man: "*Taaaahhhh*[36], forgiveness does not mean you should behave like a fool."

Me: "You are correct!"

Good man: "Forgive for your sake."

Bad man: "Your stand is correct for your sake too."

Well, this conversation went on throughout the flight, I was reeling in anger and my heart was on fire (you could boil water but not roast *bole*[37] *sha*[38]!)

All went well until we were about to land. We could see the tarmac, the tyres were about to touch the ground, when out of nowhere, the pilot picked the plane up back into the air at such a high speed, the plane was almost vertical. For a Boeing aircraft, it was shaking and struggling to pick altitude.

---

[36] No way

[37] Plantain

[38] Exclamation!

Ọmọ[39]… my life flashed before my eyes! Truly, in the face of the storm, nothing else matters. That hurt paled in the face of eternity. I was about to meet my Lord and I had the sin of unforgiveness. *gasp*

See me confessing my sins. By this time, the bad man had disappeared o!

Good man: "*Emm...* did you say you would not forgive?"
Me: "Nooooo! I forgive everybody!"

The plane was shaking like this, it was shaking like this.

Good man: "I cannot hear you."
Me: "I am sorry, I forgive from my heart… from the very bottom of my heart. In fact, I do not even remember it."

Everyone burst out in thanksgiving and prayers when we stabilized. The pilot gave one excuse of poor visibility that I did not buy. Something was about to go horribly wrong. Was I Jonah? *Amam*[40] o! But I sure felt like him!

---

[39] Boy! (Exclamation)

[40] Do I know?

A few hours after, my brother apologized but before the apology came, I had already forgiven, not half-heartedly but fully, from my heart.

Do not wait for God to teach you a lesson. Forgive for your sake. Disagreements will come but reconcile quickly and let brotherly love continue.

Be Anxious For Nothing, Including A Missing Purse

---

*Be careful(anxious) for nothing; but in
every thing by prayer and supplication with
thanksgiving let your requests be made
known unto God.*
Philippians 4:6

Celebrations such as weddings and birthdays are always something to look forward to in the Apostle Numbere family. We sure do know how to have a "Holy Ghost party", and everyone around us knows this. At one wedding, our in-laws said we were high! Literally! I assure you though, none of us is on any substance. We should actually set up an outfit so people can hire us to be the life of their *parrrryyy* (party)!

In 2019, our matriarch (my mum) was turning 70 years old, and preparations were in top gear. Myself and one of my sisters-in-law were responsible for buying the *aso-ebi* (party attire), as we were in Lagos. So, we opted to visit the famous Balogun market, which can rightly be called the market of all markets.

On the first "missionary journey", we went to scout the land. Interestingly both of us are "JJCs" (newbies), so we got lost and tried using Google maps to navigate our way out of the market. Let's just say we almost clocked 10,000 steps in our walk.

The "second missionary journey" was for shopping. I took my purse which contained every single card I have in my life: Voters card, ATM cards, driver's license, name it, it was all in there. I honestly cannot explain why I kept them all there. Just before I was to leave home, I opened the purse, and had a prompt, "What if this purse gets missing?" This is the one we say, *"my body radio me"* (I had a premonition).

I shrugged it off and went along with the purse. My sister-in-law and her relative arrived at the market. I took out the key to my house from the purse and left it in the car, hung my purse around my hand and stepped into the market.

Since we had already scouted the market, we found what we wanted very quickly and settled in the shop. I breathed a sigh of relief and brought out my paper and pen to match people and yards of material requested for. We were buying for the whole family. At this point, I took the purse off my hand and put it by my side on the long bench where I sat.

I noticed a lady with a child at her back at one end of the shop. I got up briefly and at that very moment, she stepped towards me. As it was a small shop, she brushed past me, almost pushing me down. I regained my balance, murmuring to myself about how people could not exercise patience.

I sat back in a few seconds and reached for my purse. It was gone! I screamed, eyes wide open, "My purse!". I had been robbed! We all frantically searched the shop, ran outside to see if we could find the lady with the child, but she was gone. Ahhhh!!! I was speechless! My bones were weak. All I could think of was not the little money I had in there, but all my cards.

As I paced about, I remembered the regular saying at home "Have you prayed about it?" I sat back on the bench, bent my head and prayed. I asked God to bring my purse back. I was not interested in the money – the money could go – but what I wanted were my cards. That was the prayer I said. I now understood why people go into the market without bags, or if they had to, they carried them on their chest.

Well, we finished shopping and it was a very sad Tammy that went home and told her family what happened. My husband and I prayed again, I cancelled my ATM cards and prepared to make police reports on the other missing cards.

About a week later, I got a call from my husband, he had

received a call from a stranger. Telling me that my purse was in her possession.

I screamed for joy! We connected and I went to recover the purse. Apparently, the thief had taken it to a toilet in a bank in the heart of the market. After taking the money, she left it in the toilet. The cleaner saw it and gave it to the bank personnel. This good lady while examining the purse thought to herself that she needed to reach this person. There were too many valuable cards and the owner must be in pain. She saw my next of kin, that is my husband's contact on one of them and placed a call. I am grateful to these two wonderful ladies who recovered my purse and ensured I received it.

Yep, my lost purse had been recovered after getting missing in the great Balogun market of Lagos. God answers prayers. He answered mine to a T. Next time, I will pray for the money to be recovered as well. Lessons learned; never again did I carry so many valuables at a time.

CHAPTER 24

Like Little Children

*And said, Verily I say unto you,
Except ye be converted, and become as
little children, ye shall not enter into the
kingdom of heaven.*
Matthew 18:3

My youngest daughter gave me a practical session on forgiveness some years back. Her school had an Easter show which was to start by 8AM. All through the week, she kept on practicing and showing me her moves. She was so excited. In fact, I combed the city the day before looking for her white outfit as required.

The D-Day arrived and super mum, who knows every every (that is me by the way! *flips hair*) started dragging her feet. I cannot even imagine what I was thinking. You know when you think you have time, but by the time you realize, 10 minutes have passed.

The bottom line is that we arrived 5 or 10 minutes late. That is what they said oh, but as far as I am concerned, their clock was 5 to 10 minutes fast *side eye*. As we arrived, her elder sister's class was on stage. That one jumped through the back door and joined her classmates. Unfortunately, the lower class had gone first and it was over.

My little daughter burst into tears instantly. I could hear my heart break into shimmering bits. She wailed! Tears, catarrh... ah! See me speaking big English to her teachers! "Did you say 8 or 8:30? Did you sing the National anthem?

What about the school anthem? How come her class was done?"

Ọmọ[41]… I started begging her! "I am so sorry, forgive me! Please, I am sorry!" Yep, it was my fault! Her teachers joined me to console her.

Well, I went to work and I was to pick her up after school. I just *jejely*[42] arranged my ATM card, because I was ready to buy her all the ice-cream, popcorn, name it; anything she asked for, she would get.

With my apologies in my mouth and ATM card in my hand, I went to her class. This sweet little girl jumped into my arms screaming, "Mummy!" *Huh?* *eyes wide open*. She hugged me so tight, so excited to see me! It was like NOTHING ever happened.

I saw why God said we must become like children! If it was me, hmm, I would sulk for one good week! Children bear no record of hurt, they forgive so easily.

---

[41] Boy! (Exclamation)

[42] Quietly

Second lesson learned, going forward, I made sure to be at all events 30 minutes earlier.

I got away with a clean slate with her but not so fast with her grandma! She finished me, she gave me an ear full! As she would always say, these are her grandchildren, so I should go and look for my grandma to spoil me!

The Great Surprise Plan

Love suffers long and is kind; love does not envy; love does not parade itself, is not puffed up; does not behave rudely, does not seek its own, is not provoked, thinks no evil; does not rejoice in iniquity, but rejoices in the truth; bears all things, believes all things, hopes all things, endures all things. Love never fails. But whether there are prophecies, they will fail; whether there are tongues, they will cease; whether there is knowledge, it will vanish away. For we know in part and we prophesy in part. But when that which is perfect has come, then that which is in part will be done away. When I was a child, I spoke as a child, I understood as a child, I thought as a child; but when I became a man, I put away childish things. For now we see in a mirror, dimly, but then face to face. Now I know in part, but then I shall know just as I also am known. And now abide faith, hope, love, these three; but the greatest of these is love.

1 Corinthians 13:4 – 13 (NKJV)

Our home was full of fun and laughter. Yes, there were challenging times of course but we can say the good times far outweighed the bad times. My parents were such a tag team. They could disagree in private but before us, their children, they stood together. My mum was a disciplinarian (she still is), but dad was on another level. She would handle matters but the moment she escalated to the Supreme court (that is my dad), you knew you were in for double trouble. One of those days (I do not remember the details), he read us the riot act – "This is my wife (like we were not her children) and she must be respected in this house". I can say love lived in my home.

On her 63rd birthday, my dad told me he wanted to throw her a surprise birthday party. I was staying with my parents at the time as I nursed my new baby. Surprise party? How were we going to pull this off? You see, my mum's spiritual and physical "antennas" are very sharp. She can discern people from miles away. When dad had celebrated her 50th birthday, it was meant to be a surprise but *naah*[43], it was no surprise, she could tell something was cooking.

---

[43] No

We know this, so the only time we pulled off a surprise party was at her 58th birthday. We, her children were in charge. How did we do it? She was out of the country and we fixed the party on the day of her arrival. First, she would not be in town while we made arrangements and secondly, she would not be picking phone calls outside the country because we expected some of the guests to call her and say, "Mummy, your children are wonderful o! Do you know they are planning a party for you?" Yep! That had a 99% chance of happening and ruining the surprise. It was indeed a surprise as she arrived from the airport into a party. Every other celebration, we did not even bother to try and surprise her. *Ko le work*[44]!

Fast forward to her 63rd and Apostle wanted to pull it off. We said okay. He swung into action. As the honorable chairman, surprise birthday planning committee, he made sure everyone had roles and responsibilities. He assigned himself, the task of taking her out of the house at about 3 PM just before the guests arrived. We would notify him once we were ready and they would return to the shouts of "SURPRISE!" Cool!

---

[44] It won't work

Virtually every day, he would check to see the status of things and then tell me, "I have everything sorted out, I will take her out, so no issues!" He said it with such pride and confidence that men…, my expectations were very high, I mean very high!

D-day and we were all excited. Of course, not without dad bragging about his grand plan of taking mum out of the house. 3 PM on the dot, I told him it was time. Together we went to the room where she sat, and I turned with great expectation to hear my dad unveil his plan.

"Nee, let's go to the Base", said Dad! Whattttt? Did I hear well? He said it again, "Nee, let's go to the Base". THE BASE was his top-secret, well executed, grandiose plan. Steeped in history, "The Base", is over 40 years old, located in Port Harcourt, and hosts a church, living quarters and my dad's official office. Yep! This was where he wanted to take her to and on her birthday.

Her response? "For what?" With that "Katchy" look that is best seen and not described (My mum is from the great Katchy family of Awka, Anambra State, Nigeria). Of course, she gave a big fat "NO!" I ran out of the room stifling my laughter. Plan A down the drain, both of us met outside to re-strategize. My dad said, "Do not worry, since she does not want to go out, we will detain her upstairs". Easier said than done.

In another 10 minutes, I saw the detainee on the staircase, on her way down to the laundry. I screamed! I am sure by now she had already sensed what was happening. I took the clothes from her, guided her back into the room, and frantically searched for the prison warder. Dad was in his study, reading his newspaper on duty, not realizing that there was a 'prison break'!

Well, I shared this story at the party, and we all promised to help him next time with his grand plans. We never stopped teasing him about this until he passed on.

Love is all that matters, the plans might not be perfect, but the love and the effort to show that love, is all that matters.

Nothing Prepares You For This

And said, Naked came I out of my mother's
womb, and naked shall I return thither:
the LORD gave, and the LORD hath taken away;
blessed be the name of the LORD.
Job 1:21

Pain is part of the Christian walk and life itself. However, we always believe it would never happen to us. Losing a loved one can be so painful, the pain cannot be described. I experienced so much pain when my dad passed and when I lost my twins.

I believed my dad would never die. As a matter of fact, I never even imagined it. Death did not even exist for him. We had seen God come through for him whether it was accidents or health-wise. As a matter of fact he was very healthy and took no medication until 2010. Thankfully, my mum and brother are medical doctors, so we believe in science as well.

His health began to deteriorate in 2014 and even then, death was not an option. As we struggled and battled to keep him alive, he just kept putting his house in order. We were getting frustrated, "You need to believe with us and stop saying your goodbyes". Well, God was telling us, his time was up, but we fought back. I guess, He just wanted to indulge us and kept him a little longer.

I was on my way to the airport when I got the life-changing news that he was gone. I still remember the exact spot. I almost flung the car door open. I screamed and cried. At the airport and on the plane, I just kept crying, my world was shattered. I was almost running crazy. People must have been wondering what was wrong with me.

It was another two years before I could say I really began to heal. I understood that what David did after he lost his child was no mean feat. It took a lot of strength for him to submit to God's will, and worship. It took a lot of strength for Job to bow down in worship when he lost not one, but all his adult children.

It is already so painful, people around need to be careful of what they say or do and just be supportive. The dead person can "belong" to everybody, but the people directly hit by the passing are his/her immediate family. Everyone moves on after the burial, but they are left with a gaping hole.

Well, the healing began, and I came out stronger. I took solace in God and He comforted me. Take all the time you need, it might take a while, but you will be alright.

I wrote the lines below to all my friends and family who have lost loved ones. May God comfort you the way only He can!

NOTHING PREPARES YOU FOR THIS

Nothing prepares you for this!
The deafening silence from him when you call his name
The coldness of his skin, once warm
The blankness as your heart beats faster
Yet your mind is as cold as the hands of death
Nothing prepares you for this!

Nothing prepares you for this!
The silence all around you even though you can hear
The sound of the feet of mourners as they knock on
your door
The barrage of sympathy, tears and wailing
Yet all is frightfully still and quiet
Nothing prepares you for this!

Nothing prepares you for this!
The pain you feel so deep, yet cannot be explained
The wrenching of your gut as the pain slowly pulls
The gaping hole in your heart that has no end
Yet it does not feel enough to handle reality
Nothing prepares you for this!

Nothing prepares you for this!
You can drop the facade of steel and let your guard
down
You can drop the poker face and let it all out
It might pour out like a rain of tears
It might pour out like shrill shrieks
Nothing prepares you for this!

Yes, nothing prepares you for this!
Just remember that the One who felt the most pain
holds you firmly
So, take all the time you need
It might take a while but one day at a time
The pain will pass, healing will come
For death has been swallowed up in victory!

Epilogue

As I penned down these few events in my life and the lessons I have learned, my heart was filled with gratitude. I am indeed grateful to God for every single one of them. Whether I class them as good or bad, I can safely say, they have all served their purpose. Some I might never understand God's reason for letting them happen, but one thing I understand and know is that God loves me with an everlasting love and He will never give me more than I can bear.

As I face the rest of my life and create more memories, I am excited about the future. One thing that is not in doubt is that God's thoughts for me are of peace and not of evil to give me an expected end. Therefore, I say like the songwriter, "My times are in thy hand; my God, I wish them there"

> My times are in thy hand;
> My God, I wish them there;
> My life, my friends, my soul, I leave
> Entirely to thy care.

My times are in thy hand,
Whatever they may be;
Pleasing or painful, dark or bright,
As best may seem to thee.

My times are in thy hand;
Why should I doubt or fear?
My Father's hand will never cause
His child a needless tear.

My times are in thy hand,
Jesus the Crucified;
Those hands my cruel sins had pierced
Are now my guard and guide.

Written by W. F. Lloyd Source: Trinity Hymnal (Rev. ed.) #684

In case you do not know Jesus as your Lord and Savior, I invite you to accept Him into your life. He will give your life meaning and above all, save your soul from destruction just as He did to me. Say this prayer:

Dear Lord Jesus, I know that I am a sinner, and I ask for Your forgiveness. I believe You died for my sins and rose from the dead. I turn from my sins and invite You to come into my heart and life. Be my Lord and Savior. In Jesus Name, Amen.

www.ingramcontent.com/pod-product-compliance
Lightning Source LLC
Chambersburg PA
CBHW020720160726
47993CB00006B/2286